My First Hidden Pictures
Banana Search

HIGHLIGHTS PRESS
Honesdale, Pennsylvania

So Many Shoes!

Joey is shopping for new shoes. Which should he pick?

Art by Dave Klug

Find these hidden objects in the scene.

Banana   Magnifying Glass   Paintbrush   Hairbrush

Frog   Belt   Tack   Leaf

Find the two shoes that look the same.

Play Ball!

Charlie is hoping for a home-run kick.

Art by Kenneth Spengler

Find these hidden objects in the scene.

Banana

Bell

Umbrella

Scissors

Canoe

Fork

Toothbrush

Paintbrush

Use crayons or markers to add patterns to these butterflies.

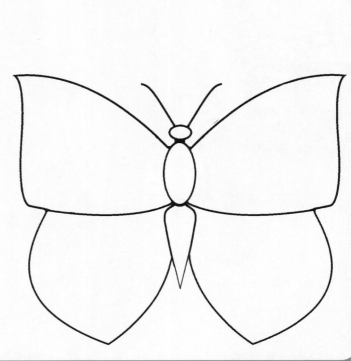

A Wheel Treat

The Ferris wheel is Chewy's favorite ride at the fair.

Art by Dave Clegg

Find these hidden objects in the scene.

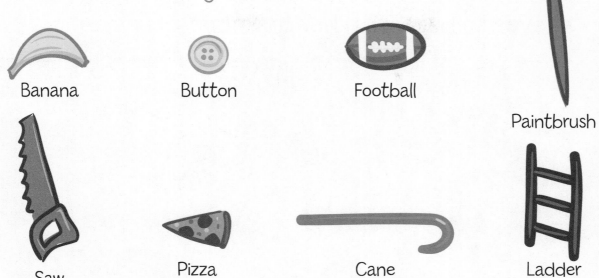

Banana

Button

Football

Paintbrush

Saw

Pizza

Cane

Ladder

Connect the dots from 1 to 23 to see a sweet treat at the fair.

Fresh Bread

Brooke loves to bake with her grandma.

Art by Mike Dammer

Find these hidden objects in the scene.

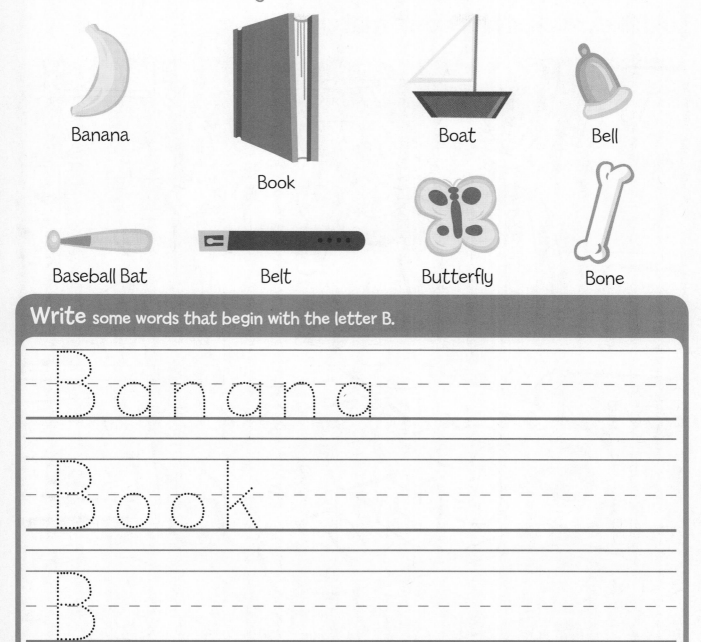

Banana

Book

Boat

Bell

Baseball Bat

Belt

Butterfly

Bone

Write some words that begin with the letter B.

Banana

Book

B

B

Good Morning!

Lulu likes socks that don't match.

Art by Kelly Kennedy

Find these hidden objects in the scene.

 Banana

 Magnet

 Fish

 Snake

 Baseball Bat

 Candle

 Paintbrush

 Toast

 Ring

Find the two sock monkeys that look the same.

Movie Night

These friends couldn't wait to see "Birds at Sea."

Art by Carolina Farias

Find these hidden objects in the scene.

 Banana

 Heart

 Paintbrush

 Baseball Bat

 Mitten

 Spoon

 Slice of Pie

 Ball of Yarn

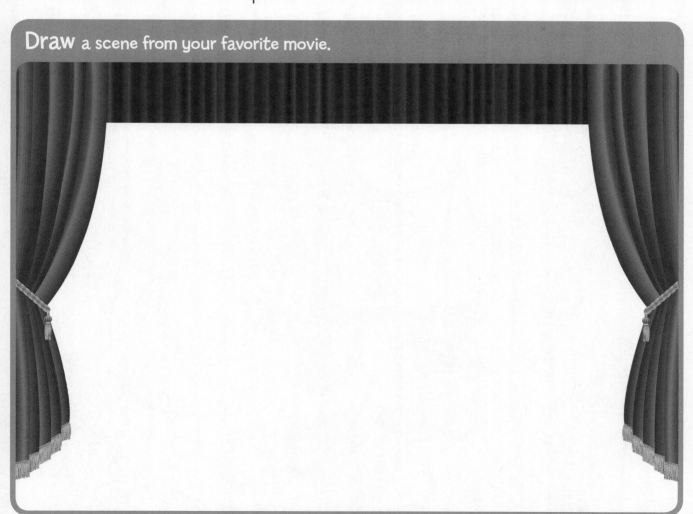

Draw a scene from your favorite movie.

Tuning Up

The band is getting ready for their show.

Find these hidden objects in the scene.

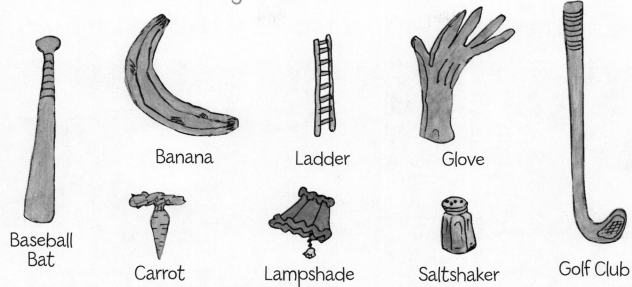

Banana

Ladder

Glove

Baseball Bat

Carrot

Lampshade

Saltshaker

Golf Club

Color each shape that has a star to see another noisemaker.

Camping Tales

Maria and her friends like to tell stories when they camp out.

Art by Kelly Kennedy

Find these hidden objects in the scene.

 Banana

 Teacup

 Glove

 Frog

 Flashlight

 Wristwatch

 Paintbrush

 Ice-Cream Cone

Follow the lines to make words.

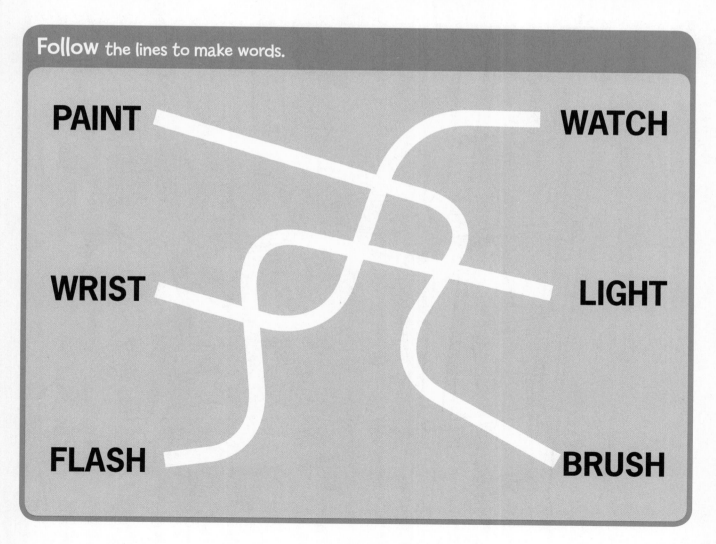

PAINT — WATCH

WRIST — LIGHT

FLASH — BRUSH

Kitty up a Tree

Mr. Jones saves the day!

Art by Ron Lieser

Find these hidden objects in the scene.

Banana

Drinking Straw

Mug

Carrot

Ice-Cream Bar

Nail

Candle

Cane

Find the two cats with yarn that look the same.

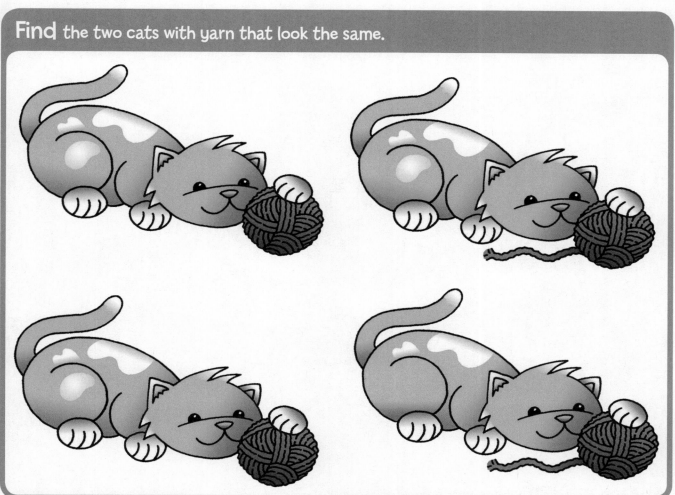

Art by Ron Lieser

Leap Frogs

Bouncy and Spot can jump really high.

Art by Dave Clegg

Find these hidden objects in the scene.

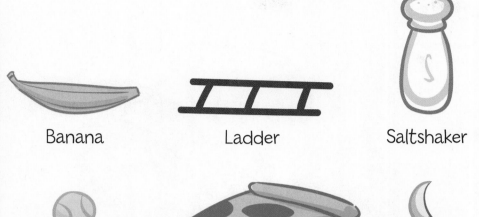

Banana   Ladder   Saltshaker   Crayon

Baseball   Pizza   Moon   Spoon

Color each shape that has a star to see another jumper.

Art by R. Michael Palan

All Aboard!

Next stop: the kitchen.

Art by Amy Wummer

Find these hidden objects in the scene.

Banana

Camera

Comb

Spatula

Purse

Ring

Snail

Lime

Connect the dots from 1 to 24 to see something a train might pull.

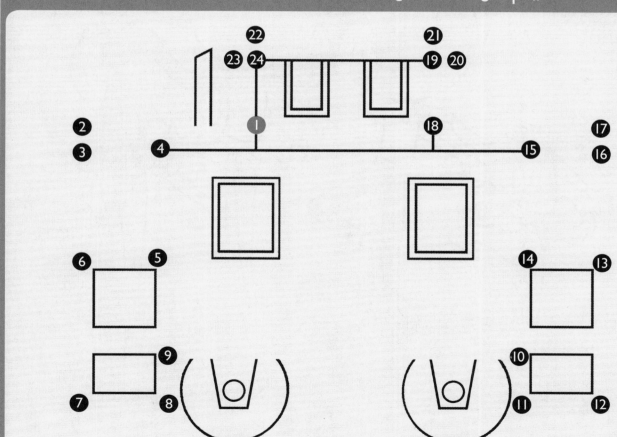

Art by Ron Lieser

Dance Moves

Anna loves ballet class.

Art by Marilyn Janovitz

Find these hidden objects in the scene.

Banana

Button

Mitten

Kite

Pencil

Drum

Flashlight

Ball of Yarn

Find the two ballet shoes that look the same.

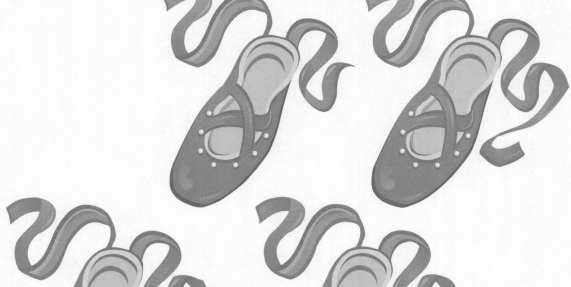

Quiet Time

These friends are reading their favorite books.

Art by Susan Detwiler

Find these hidden objects in the scene.

Banana

Feather

Bread

Kite

Lollipop

Mitten

Slice of Pie

Crayon

Connect the dots from 1 to 20 to see who's been reading *How to Bark Like a Dog.*

BARK!
BARK!

!

Balloon Fun

Bella asked for a balloon bee.

Art by Dave Klug

Find these hidden objects in the scene.

Banana

Bread

Boot

Belt

Book

Bell

Broccoli

Button

Write some words that begin with the letter B.

Bread

Bell

B

B

Party Game

It's Nathan's turn to take a swing.

Art by Sarah Beise

Find these hidden objects in the scene.

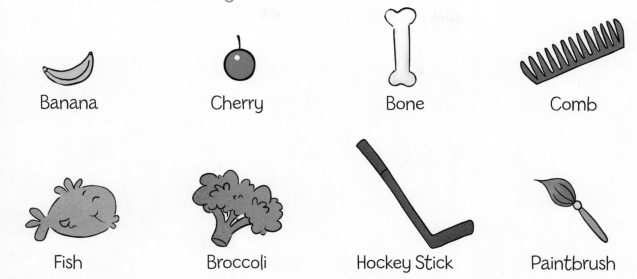

Banana

Cherry

Bone

Comb

Fish

Broccoli

Hockey Stick

Paintbrush

Use crayons or markers to add ribbons and wrapping paper.

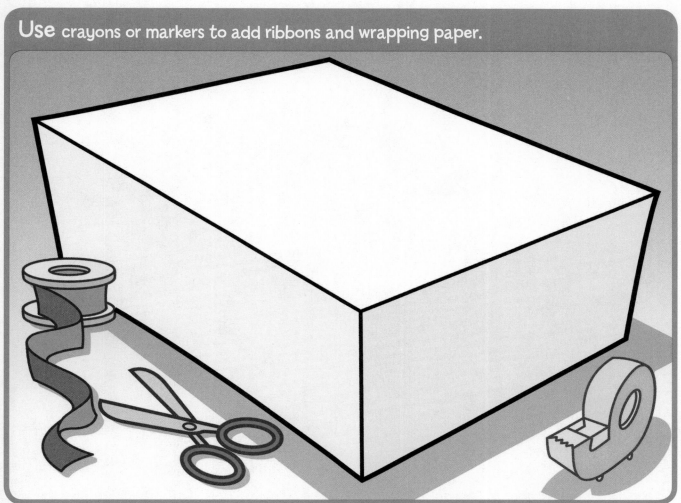

Just a Trim!

Leo is getting a haircut today.

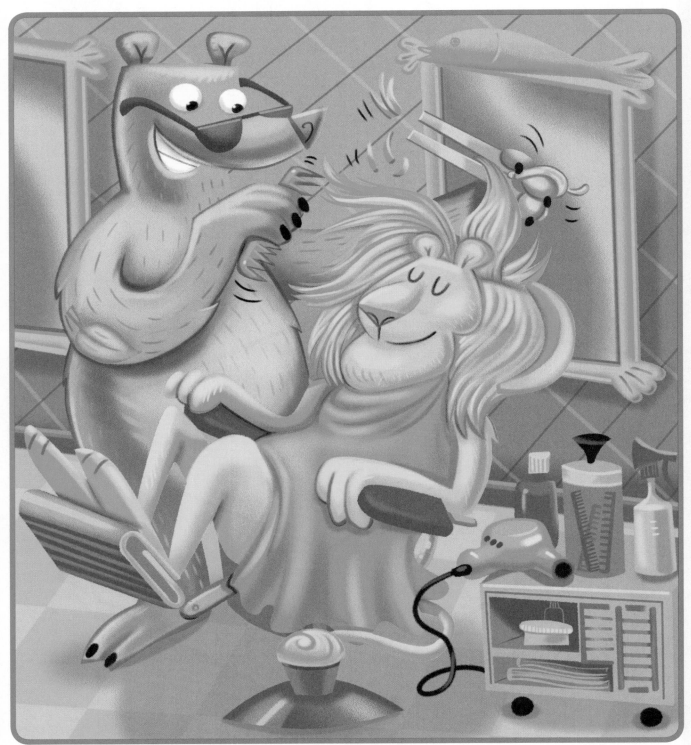

Art by Brian White

Find these hidden objects in the scene.

Banana

Ice-Cream Bar

Cupcake

Paper Clip

Leaf

Fish

Ladder

Ladle

Color each shape that has a star to see something a barber uses.

Art by R. Michael Palan

Come Out, Spot!

Jordan can't find Spot.

Art by Tammie Lyon

Find these hidden objects in the scene.

Banana

Fork

Pear

Yo-Yo

Button

Crayon

Mitten

Paper Clip

Follow the steps to draw a dog.

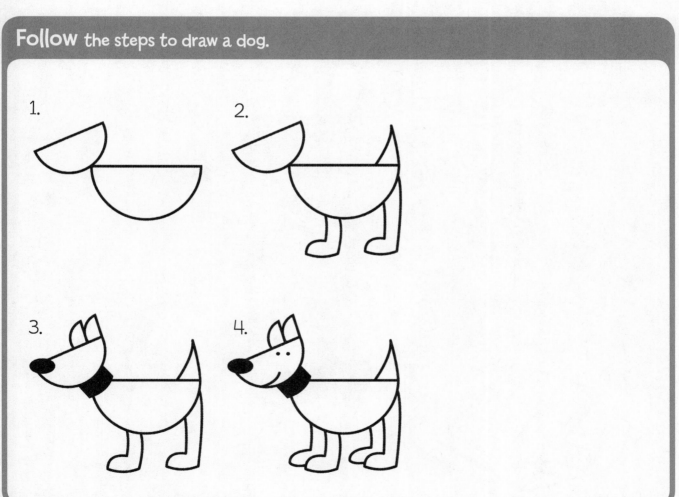

1.

2.

3.

4.

Art by Ron Zalme

Dress-Up Time

A rainy day is a good time to play in the attic.

Art by Kelly Kennedy

Find these hidden objects in the scene.

Banana

Paper Clip

Envelope

Hot Dog

Pizza

Fish

Ice-Cream Cone

Wristwatch

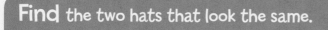

Find the two hats that look the same.

Art by Mike Dammer

37

Around We Go

It's Helga's first time on a merry-go-round.

Art by Dave Clegg

Find these hidden objects in the scene.

 Banana

 Bat

 Bell

 Golf Club

 Piece of Popcorn

Cane

 Horseshoe

 Doughnut

Color each shape that has a star to see who is waiting to ride.

Beach Volleyball

"I've got it!" yells Teddy.

Art by Robin Boyer

Find these hidden objects in the scene.

Banana

Sun

Ice-Cream Cone

Bow Tie

Acorn

Toothbrush

Cupcake

Spoon

Moon

Gift

Ruler

Envelope

Use crayons or markers to add designs to this surfboard.

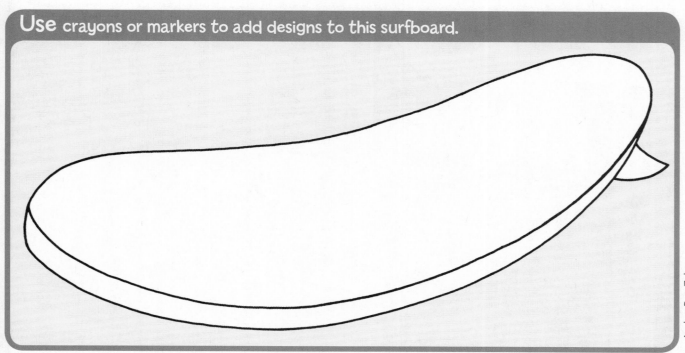

Art by Ron Zalme

Printing Paper

Benny is showing his friend how to make wrapping paper with washable paints.

Art by Jamie Smith

Find these hidden objects in the scene.

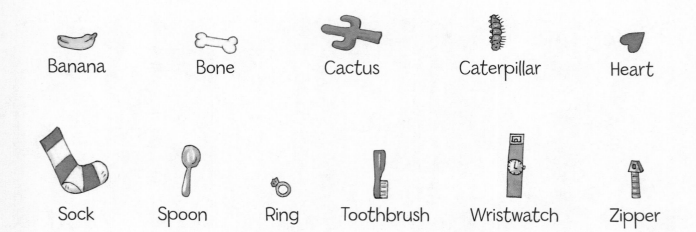

Banana   Bone   Cactus   Caterpillar   Heart

Sock   Spoon   Ring   Toothbrush   Wristwatch   Zipper

Connect the dots from 1 to 21 to see something you can use to decorate a package.

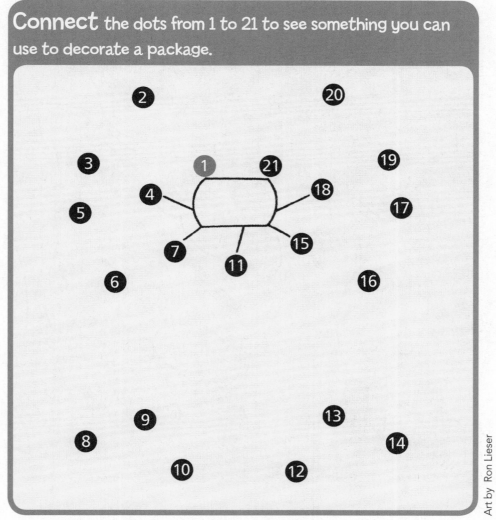

At the Vet

Oops! Fluffy got away.

Art by Dave Klug

Find these hidden objects in the scene.

Banana

Seashell

Trowel

Bell

Pineapple

Horn

Sock

Moon

Lock

Caterpillar

Feather

Draw your dream pet here.

Answers

Front Cover

So Many Shoes! pages 2-3

Play Ball! pages 4-5

A Wheel Treat pages 6-7

It's cotton candy!

Fresh Bread pages 8-9

Good Morning! pages 10-11

Movie Night   pages 12-13

Tuning Up   pages 14-15

It's a saxophone!

Camping Tales   pages 16-17

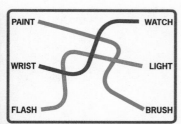

Paintbrush
Wristwatch
Flashlight

Kitty up a Tree   pages 18-19

Leap Frogs   pages 20-21

It's a bunny!

All Aboard!   pages 22-23

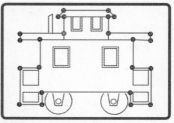

It's a caboose!

Answers

Dance Moves pages 24-25

Quiet Time pages 26-27

It's a cat!

Balloon Fun pages 28-29

Party Game pages 30-31

Just a Trim! pages 32-33

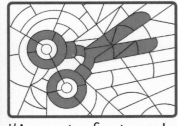

It's a pair of scissors!

Come Out, Spot! pages 34-35